PUSH Promote Until Shipping and Handling

By

Sophisticated Press LLC

PUSH: Promote Until Shipping and Handling

Published by Sophisticated Press LLC

Edited By: Destini Hall

Book Cover Design Sophisticated Press LLC

PRINTED IN THE UNITED STATES OF AMERICA

ISBN 978-0-9988669-6-3

SP

SOPHISTICATED
PRESS

This book is dedicated to the employee that is ready for the transition to Entrepreneurship.

"Every Business should have a book and every book is a Business."

- Renetta Gunn-Stevens

Table of Contents

Introduction 1

Finding Your Super Power 2

Locating Your Why 7

Finding Your Readers 18

How To Introduce Your Manuscript Into the Marketplace 31

How to Create a Variety of Content 36

Pre-Order Campaigns 39

How To Sell Without Selling 56

Creating a Street Team 70

Profits Over Popularity 76

Interviews and Podcasts Etiquette 79

Shipping & Handling With Care 84

25 *PUSH* Tips 86

15 Ways To *PUSH* Your Book 89

About the Author 90

Introduction

Hello and thank you for purchasing *PUSH*: Promote Until Shipping and Handling. This book was written for writers, authors, and entrepreneurs in hopes that you will operate your book like a business. In fact that is our motto, "Every Business should have a book, and every book is a Business." Our goal is to equip you with the confidence and resources that are needed to *PUSH* correctly in the Publishing Marketplace. After assisting a surplus of Authors with self-publishing tasks, we identified that there was an area of opportunity for marketing training. Authors had mastered writing and self-publishing but failed at social media, sales, and promoting. We could not allow our fellow writer's demise. Immediately Sophisticated Press began creating a quick reference guide for the Authors that wanted to solve this incompetency. Grab your notebook and let's begin the journey of learning how to *PUSH*.

Renetta Gunn-Stevens,

CEO, Sophisticated Press LLC

Finding Your Super Power

"Every child is an artist. The problem is how to remain one when you grow up."

Pablo Picasso

When you hear the term *Super Power* it's referring to your strengths and skills that make you unique or that assist you to dominate in your field of expertise. Many believe you will be successful if you are blending with the masses. In reality your uniqueness will distinguish you from the crowd. Being peculiar gives you the advantage. At first it will feel awkward, intimidating, and rebellious. No worries, keep being your authentic self unapologetically.

We are all born with a unique *Super Power*. Your *Super Power* will surface when you arrive to the proper environment. Finding your *Super Power* is a matter of answering some very specific questions.

One method to utilize in finding your *Super Power* is to replay all of the compliments you have received over your life span. Look for the following recurrences:

- Which praises have you received in duplicates?

- What is the consistent compliment your Supervisor, co-workers, or friends have given you?

A fish will always look foolish, desperate, and frantic out of water. If you put the fish into the water their inner genius surfaces. No one taught the fish how to swim in the water. The fish was born with that skill. It's in their DNA to breathe underwater. Could it be you look and feel misplaced because you are in the wrong environment?

Have you ever been lost? When you are lost, what is the first action you take? You look around for someone to ask a question. When you are lost in your identity you have to do the same thing, ask questions.

Former CEO of Google, Eric Schmidt (2001-2011) quoted, "We built this company on questions, not answers."

Questions matters! If you don't ask the right question you won't receive the correct answer. Questions help to identify the gaps in information or understanding. Your questions also reveal your level of comprehension.

What are the questions you are asking yourself to find your *Super Power?*

Questions to Ask Yourself to Find Your "Super Power"

1. What was your hobby as a child?

2. What or who did you want to become before you grew up and responsibilities changed your mind?

3. What subject do you have a massive accumulation of knowledge of?

4. What skills can you do effortlessly that others struggle with?

5. How do you amaze people?

6. What field or environment are you fearless in?

Questions For The Marketplace

1. Is there a void in the Marketplace for your *Super Power*?

2. What uniqueness are you bringing to the Marketplace?

3. What tier of clients will your *Super Power* serve?

4. Do you have a track record of using your *Super Power* and getting results? If so, you want to enter this data in your manuscript.

Now that you have located your skill trait that is dominant, how do we apply it to the *PUSH*. First you have to embrace your *Super Power*. We expect our *Super Power* to come with flashing lights and a siren. Your *Super Power* could possibly be visible and you find it hard to accept because we tend to complicate things. Remember the simple is very profound.

There are three benefits of knowing your Super Power:

1. You fully understand what environment brings your genius out and *PUSH* you to dominate.

2. You get to help others find their *Super Power*.

3. People pay you for using your *Super Power* to solve problems.

Locating Your Why

So you want to write a book? Why? No seriously, why? Now before you answer this question think about it. Your answer will determine how much passion you have. Your passion will determine how well you will perform in the process of self-publishing a book. People publish books for a plethora of reasons. Some Authors write a book in honor of a love one. Others write a book because that is the only method of getting their side of a story heard. Many write books to build a career in. They hope to one day see their manuscript on the "Big Screen". There is a professional arena of leaders that write books to educate their consumer base/clients or enhance their brand's identity. Optimistic people write hoping to get rich overnight.

As you can see there are many reasons to write a book and none of them are right or wrong. As long as the writer has a clear expectation, there will be no disappointments.

Show me a person without their "why" and we will witness a person who won't be able to endure the process. Show me a person who understands their "why" and we will witness an executor.

My rule of thumb is to always identify the "why" before taking on any big tasks.

If you are on the fence of publishing here is a list to help you make a decision.

Questions to Ask When Discovering Your "Why" for Publishing?

1. Are you self-publishing with the expectation of becoming a New York Times Best Seller?

2. Are you writing to become an Amazon Best Seller?

3. Is the book your publishing a keepsake item?

4. Will the information inside your book enhance other people's lives?

5. Are you writing this book out of revenge or hurt?

6. Does the content in the manuscript cause humiliation to others?

7. Will the content in your book assist you in your career progression?

8. Are you writing a book simply for KUDOS?

9. Does your book have an audience that is requesting the data?

10. What problem does your book solve for the reader?

Often times an Author's "Why" for publishing is to hurt the person who hurt them. For instance, they want to tell their story of abuse to expose a love one or abuser. If this is your approach, make sure that you have had counseling to heal from the trauma and consider publishing your book to help and heal. How do you change the narrative? You write from the position of a victor rather than a victim. Always seek legal counseling if you are going to expose violent or illegal actions, people names, and accusations that are against the law but have not been reported to law enforcements.

Sometimes there is a fear that comes upon you when you are writing a book. Join writing communities so you are around like minded people.

10 Reasons To Publish A Book

1. Books add credibility to your products or services.

2. Distinguish you from your colleagues and counterparts in your industry.

3. Adds value to your brand.

4. Adds respect to your name.

5. Adds an additional stream of income.

6. Makes your Super Power is accessible to the world.

7. Books bridge to opportunities for conferences, trainings, and workshops.

8. Helps build a relationship with your client base.

9. Adds value to your network.

10. Establish you as an expert in the Marketplace.

Take a few moments and think about the benefits. Ponder to see if these benefits are beneficial to you.

A person can publish a book for a variety of reasons. The intent of this book is to help writers that are self-publishing enhance their life but more importantly others. Writing a successful book requires dedication. You have to sacrifice a lot of yourself. Don't believe me? Wait and see. When you have resolutions for the masses, it's not easy to stay quiet or keep the information contained.

- Would you see a pothole and not tell the pedestrian that is about to fall in it?

- Would you know the answer or resolution to dilemma that someone is facing and not provide the insight?

Most decent human beings that have the capacity to help will offer it.

This is how I found my "why" to write this book. As a Publisher I witness many Authors jumping into publishing without knowing their "why". This is why they are not able to endure the whole process of writing.

Before the manuscript is packaged in the book cover there is work to do. After the manuscript is in the Marketplace that same work is due and even more.

What is that work you ask? You have to *PUSH*. I'm not talking about physically shoving tangible objects or people. When I ask you to *PUSH* I am asking you to promote until shipping & handling takes place. DO NOT STOP until you are shipping off manuscript copies around the world.

Merriam-Webster dictionary defines the word promotion as the publicization and informing of a product, organization, or venture so as to increase sales or public awareness. The word promote means further the progress of (something, especially a cause, venture, or aim); support or actively encourage.

The goal for promoting a book is to increase sales and the exposure of the content. Promotions encourage your readers to purchase.

PUSH is a mindset that is needed for the success of self-publishing. *PUSH* was created for the confident and the communicative writers. It's ok if you are not there yet. By the end of this book you will be an expert *PUSH*ER!

How to Position Yourself to *PUSH*

1. Find a *PUSH* expert in your genre and follow them on all social media channels.

2. Listen to the expert's advice.

3. Implements all of the strategies that they share that are FREE and obtainable.

4. Come out of your comfort zone.

5. Embrace all the delegated stretch assignments like Facebook LIVES and face your fears.

6. Be willing to invest in learning how to *PUSH*.

All books fall into categories known as genre. Knowing your genre will assist you in determining what type of writer you are. You don't want to be the new kid on the literary block at the wrong address. Each genre has a culture or standards. Here are a few basic genres in writing:

- Literary Fiction (Created stories).

- Thriller (Action filled stories).

- Nonfiction (Based on true story or findings).

- Science Fiction Genre includes: (Technology innovations, visions of the future, etc.)

- Horror (Scary, spiritual, hauntings)

- Poetry

- Romance

- Young Adults (YA) Written for teenagers.

- Children (Illustrations)

If you are writing a Children's book you would not study a *PUSH* expert in the genre of Horror.

The goal is to locate a successful author in your genre and learn from the Marketing strategies they are incorporating in the Marketplace.

Here is a caveat. If you are going to receive information from an expert please incorporate the directions. There is no room for excuses only EXECUTION.

After you have established your genre you will need to know the category of your book along with certain keywords.

- **Be precise.** Choose the exact categories based on the content of your book. Don't choose categories that are not identical to your topic.

- **Be detailed.** Choose individual categories instead of general ones. Readers looking for specific topics will be able to locate your book without interruption.

Produce a list of 5-7 keywords and incorporate these words into the product description headline, book descriptions, and keyword sections on each retailer product page.

Establishing the correct keywords will increase your chances of being listed on the retailer bestseller charts for a specific category. This step position the likelihood of higher sales. Keywords also prevent disappointing your readers who were expecting something different.

Amazon KDP has a great online instructional sheet available. https://kdp.amazon.com/en_US/help/topic/G200652170#choose

Finding Your Readers

Why do writers publish books? Hopefully, they publish for someone to read it. But not just anyone. Authors write for the reader that would benefit from the story, expertise, or information. In order for the writer and reader to find each other, the author has to make their book locatable. In the Marketplace your reader is labeled as the niche market.

Before you determine your niche market or your ideal reader you should determine the genre of the manuscript. In the previous chapter we listed some of the genres in literature. Knowing your genre will help build a profile of your reader behaviors and preferences. This is the first step to the *PUSH* process.

Once your genre is established, the best place to start locating readers is at home and in your contact book. Many of your family and friends are going to be excited that you have embarked on a writing journey. They won't mind purchasing a copy or giving you a shout out on their social media page.

Once your family and friends are on board it's time to focus on your professional social media following. Here is where you will need to incorporate some PUSH strategies. Your existing followers on social media are valuable to your book. Don't overlook or underestimate their like, follow, and share. Your social media followers are familiar with your voice and content and will provide a great foundation to build off of. A social relationship has already been established. These connections will be vital to the expanding of your brand and exposure to your book. The next page will review questions to ask your readers to understand their purchasing decisions.

10 Questions to Answer About Your Reader

1. Does your reader have:

    a. An illness?

    b. A criminal record?

    c. A disability?

    d. An Addiction?

2. What is your reader:

    a. Age?

    b. Gender?

    c. Religion?

    d. Sexual preference?

    e. Relationship status?

3. What is your reader?

    a. Salary?

    b. Education?

    c. Political View?

4. Is your reader:

   a. Mother

   b. Father

   c. Only child

5. Where do your reader go for recreation:

   a. Library?

   b. Concerts?

   c. Conferences?

   d. Night Clubs?

   e. Parents house?

6. Is your reader:

   a. Married?

   b. Single?

   c. Divorced?

   d. Widow?

7. How does your reader prefer to read their books:

   a. Online?

b. eBooks?

c. Paperback?

d. Audio?

8. What is your reader's preference to receive news:

a. TV?

b. Cellphone?

9. How often does your reader:

a. Vacation?

b. Move their family to different locations?

10. What are your readers favorite:

a. Food?

b. Celebrity?

c. TV Show?

d. Car?

e. Restaurant?

Once you have established who your reader is you must create a content strategy that will attract them to your book. How do you do that? You incorporate social media and the findings from the questions on the list. In the next chapter we will discuss further on how to utilize Social Media for promoting your books.

If your family and friends are not your ideal reader (niche) please don't get offended if they don't purchase a copy of your book. Let's face it, if 25 of your close family members purchased your book you would still need more sales to be an Amazon Best seller and New York Times Best Seller. So don't sever relationships over book purchases with friends and family. You need the world to support your manuscript. Think BIGGER.

Now that you have identified your niche market it's time to understand their "Why" for purchasing and supporting authors. What makes a reader purchase a book? How does a reader choose an author to support or follow? How can your manuscript become magnetic to the readers of the world? To answer the previous questions, it's time for research.

Research will allow you to go deeper into the thinking, behavior and reasoning of your niche market.

Research allows you to internally understand what makes a reader support you once, multiple times or never.

3 Strategies to Find Your Reader

1. Surveys
2. Feedback forms
3. Respond to DM, IM, & Emails

Surveys

Surveys are a great way to learn more about your readers and their preference of spending for books.

Surveys help you better understand what your readers are looking for in a book and interaction with an author. There are two types of surveys. You have long and short style surveys.

Surveys does not always bring in great responses. There are however a few tricks that you can incorporate to make it work in your interest.

Keep surveys short. No one has time for a ten minute survey these days. Try to keep your survey within five minutes. In order to execute the 5 minute rule you should not have over five questions on your survey.

Always start your survey with an open end question? Each question should be intentional. Don't waste time or data. Only ask questions that are needed and necessary for the building of a relationship with the reader.

If you have a website and you should, you can insert the survey there. The website survey should be no more than three questions. Again, readers don't have ten minutes to fill out surveys unless there are tangible rewards attached.

Surveys are comparison to appetizer in the meal. It's just the beginning stage. Next we move on to feedbacks.

Feedback

Feedback forms are necessary for customer service and product improvement. Do you have a system in place for feedback? If a reader has a bad or great experience do they know how to contact you?

Your niche will always have great suggestions on how to make their experience better. Trust me you want to hear them. These are your supporters who will give you FREE advertisement so you definitely want it to be positive versus negative.

If you don't have a feedback form, your readers will take their comments to social media. With a feedback form you have an opportunity to speak directly with your supporter and thank them or correct their issue.

Your feedback form should be visible and simple. Don't make your reader take a quiz. Simply have a form to rate their experience and provide any additional comments if needed. Once you have your feedback form in place it's important to respond to the feedback. A good turnaround time is 24-48 hours.

5 Questions to Ask on Your Feedback Form

For Purchasing Experience:

How easy or difficult was it to complete your purchase?

To Highlight Strengths:

What would you tell your friends or colleagues about this book?

Resolution:

What challenge or problem does my book solve for you?

Marketing:

How did you find out about the book (Add title)?

Introduce new feature in the market:

What value is placed on [new feature/product/service]?

After establishing a feedback system it's now time to respond accordingly. Readers usually communicate through:

- Emails

- DM (Instagram)

- IM (FB Messenger).

- Social Media posts

Responding to readers directly builds a relationship that is personal and customizable. If you really want to go the extra mile, pick up the phone and call the reader. How awesome would it be to speak directly to someone who has supported you and taken the time out of their day to provide feedback?

There is a new trend in communicating with your readers. Instant messaging is the best communication strategy for the following reasons:

1. You get instant access.

2. It's casual and not stuffy.

3. You build a relationship and rapport.

If you have a mass amount of readers in one state, wow them by having a lunch and learn to hear how your book has affected their lives.

There are a variety of ways to find your readers. We only highlighted the top four ways. You want to reach your reader before they go to social media to complain, should this occur.

Always stay in a *PUSH* state. Create engagement and excited about your book in every opportunity life provides.

How To Introduce Your Manuscript Into the Marketplace

Now that you know your "Why" for self-publishing, the genre of your manuscript has been selected, and how to reach your reader it's time to create a strategy for your brand introduction into the Marketplace.

The goal is to make your brand memorable by attaching an emotion to their interaction with your brand. How do you plan on getting the attention of readers and influencers? What is the emotion you want your niche to feel when they engage with your book/brand?

Don't make the mistake of letting fear and perfection stop you from beginning your 90 day Pre-order phase for your book, products, or services. Too many times we mentor authors that want to wait until they have the book in their hands before they start marketing. Or they will express concerns of copyright infringements so they don't include their followers on social media in the process of creation. Distrust is the wrong position to enter in a relationship. Remove fear and perfection out of your consciousness before we begin learning how to create a buzz for your book.

You will feel vulnerable at times but trust your training, gut, supporters, and most of all the experts!

Start relationships with positive and realistic expectations.

How to Introduce Your Brand Into The Marketplace

1. Identify your niche market.

2. Identify where they hang out on Social Media and meet them there with marketing.

3. Create a wide variety of content to establish yourself as a Subject Matter Expert (SME).

Elevator Pitch

A good elevator pitch last 30 seconds or less. Write a brief, quick elevator pitch that informs what the book is about, what kind of mental state readers will be engaged in, why readers should care, and what awards the book and author have received. A strong elevator pitch help readers decide whether or not to purchase your book.

Here are four questions to answer when creating your elevator pitch for your book to grab attention.

1. Who are you (AUTHOR)?

2. What does your book do? Does it inform, entertain, or enlighten.

3. What's the value proposition?

4. Offer them to read more or come along for the journey.

This elevator pitch is not effective when:

- It's too long

- The Author spends too much time talking about himself

- No call to action (CTA) is present

- Lacking attention-grabbing facts

This elevator pitch is effective when:

- It asks a question

- It reminds you of pain points

- It displays empathy

- It's straightforward

How to Create a Variety of Content

When creating content for your book ask the following question. What pain points and problems do your readers have that you can address in marketing?

How can you hear the pain points of your readers? You listen to their pain through:

- Social media posts

- Questions

- Memes.

After you have heard the problem, then you analyze the resolutions you have in products and services. The next step is to promote resolutions.

This is very important because some think promoting is all about blabbering out all the solutions your book offers. No one wants to hear all your solutions and features. They want the feature and solution that will solve their problems.

When presenting your brand, be cognizant of tone and personality. Establish brand consistency with color schemes, stock images, and fonts.

Don't change your brand yearly. You want your readers to remember your brand, recognize your brand, and select your brand over other brands. If you want more assistance with this incorporation, apply to our online self-publishing course at www.spaa.thinkific.com.

Once the pain points of your readers are revealed, here are ways to present your content:

1. Share customer testimonials. Reviews help others to build confidence that you are qualified to resolve problems.

2. Share compelling stories.

Storytelling is a very important marketing strategy to apply in promotions. This form of communication will engage your reader and influence them to make decisions in your brand favor. Good Storytelling should include graphs, charts, and end in strong call to actions.

3. Be humorous.

Find memes and other funny content that will make your readers laugh. Stay on top of trending topics and create posts that are relevant to the social wave.

Pre-Order Campaigns

A good pre-order promotion starts 90 days before launching.

Here is a list of must haves:

1. Book Cover

2. Reviews

3. Website

4. E-Commerce

For some new authors this is a time where it can get a little confusing. You are probably thinking no one will purchase your book without the physical copy being ready, but that is furthest from the truth. No one will purchase your book if you don't *PUSH*.

The truth is readers purchase books all the time based on the following features:

- Book Cover

- Reviews

- Price

All of the features can be promoted online without a physical copy of the book. A major element of *PUSH* is to make sure your product and services are packaged for success. Answer this question. What is more significant, the content or the cover?

Both!

But, before the reader can get to the content they are met by the book cover.

Book Cover

Too many times an Author will try to create their book covers by themselves and the outcome usually is low book sales and hurt feelings. There are templates available and it's very tempting to make this a DIY project but don't do it. Studies show that readers give each book about six seconds in determining if they want to pick it up and engage more. What is the determining factor? The Book Cover and the Sales Copy on the back of the book. We strongly suggest hiring a professional Graphic Designer.

Create a budget from $100-$1500 for a professional book cover.

Psychology of Color

Gold -Warmth

Orange -Friendly & Cheerful

Red- Bold & Excitement

Purple- Creative, Royal, & Wise

Blue- Dependable, Executive, Communicative, & Strength

Green- Growth & Health

Gray- Balance, Neutral, & Sadness

Benefits of a Professional Book Cover

1. Adds credibility to the content inside. If your book has low resolution pictures and fonts your reader won't take the content seriously.

2. Art Appeal. Readers want to have the freedom to read your book or place it on a cocktail table and it enhances the décor of the room.

3. Longevity in the Marketplace. Your book is competing against millions of book covers. In order for it to become successful and available on multiple platforms there has to be a demand for it by your readers. This demand will have distributors flooding your email with book orders, which in turn will keep your book in purchasing rotation.

Whether you choose a professional graphic designer or not you must choose your book dimension. The most common size for books are 6X9. However, this is not the only size available for manuscript or content.

Here is a list of dimensions in inches for conventional books in the Publishing Industry:

- Standard Paperback 6X9

- Pocket book 4.25 x 6.88

- Letter 8.5 X 11

- Children Books 8.5 X 8.5

FREE BOOK COVER SOFTWARES

1. Canva

2. Adobe Spark

3. GIMP

The software above are what we personally use for our clients. Are there other software available? Absolutely. Utilize Google search engine to explore!

The goal of the book cover is to attract the reader's eye and connect emotionally. This can be done by using great images and the right color. The book cover objective should be to get the reader to click the BUY NOW button.

Imagery

Should you decide to create your book cover on your own please use professional pictures. Is there a chance that others in the industry may have the same photo? Absolutely. But better to have a photo that is strong and compelling than unique and weak. Here is a list of FREE Stock Images sites:

- Pexels

- Unsplash

- Burst

- Pixabay

- FoodiesFeed

- Freestork.org

- Picography

- Stocksnap.io

- Canva

Fonts Matter!

Sometimes writers want to have pretty cursive fonts on their book cover. Each genre has a visual, vibe, and voice which is communicated through the book cover. Look at the following examples.

Fonts Matter

Fonts Matter

Fonts Matter

Fonts Matter

Notice how each font gives off a different tone, energy or expression. They are all 12 point font but some versions look smaller and other looks bigger. Each font will communicate to a certain audience.

Book Cover Design Websites

1. FIVERR

2. Canva

3. Upwork

4. Reedsy

When hiring a graphic designer make sure to ask for multiple versions of the book cover. A good amount is three different versions. This will help you choose the best option for your production. Remember to determine which book cover speaks to the reader pain points.

Create a survey and test your book cover with an audience. This strategy can be executed by sharing with your social media followers and have them vote!

The Anatomy of a Book

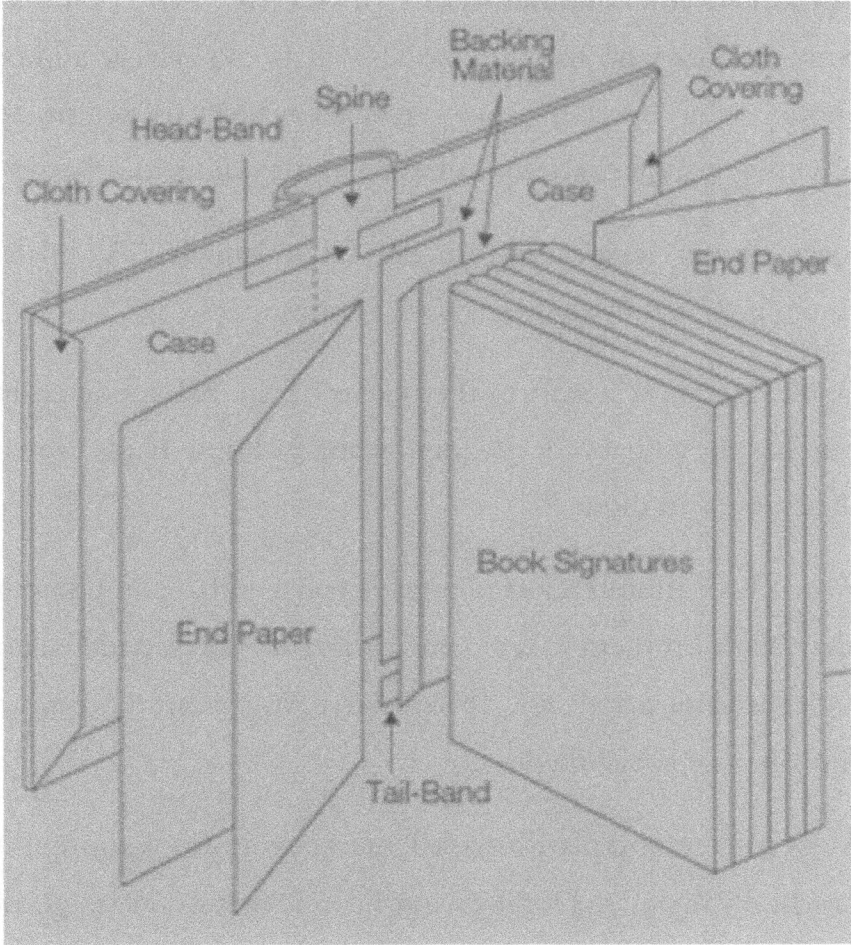

Reviews

Book reviews are written, verbal, or video recorded opinions from readers who has purchased your books. Every author should value book reviews. It helps readers to determine how they may feel after purchasing and reading your book.

Start getting reviews before the book launch, TV hosts, Radio personalities, and magazine committees.

Book reviews will inform the reader of the risk involved in purchasing your book. Readers want to know if it's worth their time and dime.

As a rule of thumb if a reader gives you a verbal compliment always ask for them to text, email, or make a 30 second video with the same accolades. If they agree, you want to promote this on your social media sites.

Most distribution platforms will market your book more if it has book reviews. Don't create false reviews. Create good work and *PUSH*!

PUSH your latest book on your website by updating the header or banners of your homepage to increase awareness. Consider including excerpts instead of a synopsis to engage visitors.

Websites

Every author should have an Author Landing Page. This is an intimate virtual meeting platform for your readers to purchase your book and provide feedback. Create your book cover in this sequence.

- Create your Author Landing Page

- Incorporate and eCommerce Store

- Start Pre-order Campaign immediately

As orders for the book comes in it will obligate you to finish the manuscript.

First step is to purchase your domain name. Every author should own their name as a domain. For example, thenameofyourbusiness.com and yourname.com. You have to decide as the author do you want to name the website after the book or the author.

The cost for a website designer can cost you between $250-$5000. You want to keep the cost as low as possible. Always ask for references of previous sites that the designer has created. Most Author Landing Pages require three tabs which are the Home, About, and Contact page.

A strong call to action (CTA) is needed for the Home page. This is a button or bold font that says Buy Now, Pre-order, Signup, etc. It's very important to receive the visitor email address that visited your site. Add an email capture app to your site to assist you with collecting the email.

Domain Purchasing Sites

1. GoDaddy.com

2. Weebly.com

3. Yahoosmallbusiness.com

4. Wix.com

5. Bluehost.com

6. Squarespace.com

7. Sitebuilder.com

eCommerce

eCommerce is a virtual platform where consumers buy and sell online. The Internet provides a quick and simple way for people to purchase your products and services without having to visit an actual brick and mortar store.

An online store gives you access to customers everywhere in the world. In fact, many readers prefer buying books online without visiting a physical location. eCommerce also has to capacity to allow you to present your book in the digital media such as eBooks and audio versions. There are a plethora of eCommerce companies, and it's important to choose a platform that allows your readers to have an user friendly experience.

Fraud protection and Secure Socket Layer (SSL) encryption should be present. The icon should be visible so readers feel secure making an online purchase. SSL technology allows online payments securely and is a must-have for your Author Landing Page.

Please Note:

- Cashapp is not an official banking system for your bookkeeping.

- Zelle is not a banking system for your book keeping.

- Your PayPal email address should be your name or match your brand.

- Establish a Business bank account with your EIN.

- Consider investing in a P.O. Box for correspondence and donations.

How To Sell Without Selling

For clarity you will need to learn how to sell when you become an Author. Sales is a vital skill to have especially if you are self-publishing your book. After all, no one should be able to sell your manuscript better than you, the creator. Salesmen sometimes get a bad rep because maybe you brought a lemon (a raggedy car) before. Perhaps maybe you purchased some perfume before that didn't even smell good and you felt con after the person was done with the deal.

I remember I was persuaded to pay $100 to join a Facebook Group. At first I was so angry but then I decided to dissect what took place on the phone call. I asked myself the following questions:

1. What phrases did the sales person use that made me feel comfortable enough to swipe my card?

2. Did they offer the sell at the beginning of the call or did they allow me to speak?

3. How effective was their compliments to my thoughts and goals?

4. Were they confident or did they seem nervous?

5. Did I feel rushed?

After studying the call I realized that getting angry was not the right response. Instead of accepting a loss of $100, I learn a sales lesson that I experienced firsthand.

We all can agree that salesmen and women should have integrity. Consider taking a sales course or connect with a mentor to teach you sales. For now we are going to cover a few sales strategies that you can apply immediately with your book marketing campaigns.

Six Ways To Sell Without Selling

1. Provide FREE content.

2. Provide content without taking rejection personal.

3. Promote through email signatures.

4. Don't provide the solution prior to knowing the problem.

5. Collaborate with INFLUENCERS.

6. Know the statistics of sales.

Provide FREE content

The old sales attitude was that your reader needed you more than you needed them. That ideal is furthest from the truth. I believe that, "A book is a prison of words waiting for the reader to set them free."

In order for your book to become a potential candidate for purchasing, the author has to begin marketing themselves as an expert in the genre. How do you establish yourself as an expert? You begin to provide free resources and information about the subject matter of your book.

Think about the industry you are in and post daily on your social media platforms, blogs, email campaigns, or podcasts informing your readers about industry updates.

Provide Marketing Without Taking Rejection Personal

Your readers or supporters won't always respond to your first attempt of sale. It's very easy to get offended when family and friends don't react to your business promotions. Don't take it personal. Remember, if everyone in your family purchased a book, your book would still not make the Best Seller list because you need more than 25 sales of your book.

Don't write a book and hold your family hostage to purchase it.

Don't write a book and expect for all your friends to support it.

Honestly if your family does not fit your niche market is it fair to expect them to support your book?

An effective promotion requires repetition that must go out to everyone regardless if the last attempt ended in an "no" or unanswered inquiries. Remember don't take it personal it's just business. Don't lose friends or family members over one sale.

Promote Through Email Signatures

Email is a method of exchanging communications using an electronic device according to Wikipedia.

Emails are very important to your pre-order campaign and your relationship with your readers. Emails can be used for the following methods:

1. Providing Updates

2. Offering Products

3. Building 'Buzz" about your book

4. Building a community

5. Communication outside of Social Media

As a rule of thumb you should have your product, service, or book links in the email signature of your communications.

A functioning website should have an email capture pop up when readers visit.

Remember you want to build a relationship which requires more than one interaction. Emails are a great way to begin a relationship building.

If you want to build a relationship with your clients keep an excel spreadsheet with the following information:

1. Name

2. Email

3. State

4. DOB

5. Signup date

Here are a few more features that you can include in your email signature:

1. Schedule appointments

2. Subscribe to YouTube Channel

3. Join email list for updates

TOP Email Platforms

1. Mailchimp

2. Constant Contact

3. Drip

4. Convert Kit

5. Keap

Don't Provide The Solution Without Knowing The Problem.

When promoting your book, it's very important to identify what problem or pain point your reader will resolve from your book, product, or services.

It does your business and expertise a disservice to just blabber off about how great your book is to readers. When you are applying the *PUSH* method you should be listening and reading your niche market concerns that they share on social media.

A good promoter knows how to listen with their ears and eyes. In order to understand your readers or niche market you have to hang out where they share their problems.

People share their problems all day on social media. You see them every day through their updates, questions, memes, status, and pictures.

Five Ways To Find Out Reader Problems

1. Read their post updates.

2. Read their responses to other post inquiries.

3. Study their memes.

4. Listen to them so you can offer the features of your book, product, or service that will resolve their problems.

5. Ask them.

Collab With INFLUENCERS

(Please look up the Federal Trade Commissions (FTC) rules on using INFLUENCERS)

What is an Influencer? An Influencer is a person who has the ability to accumulate followers and persuade them to purchase books, products, or services that they promote. In exchange for promoting, the Influencers receive a financial incentive for their marketing.

In marketing it's not a secret strategy to utilize celebrity endorsements to render profits and an increase in sales. Everyone can't afford to pay a celebrity thousands or even hundreds of dollars to endorse their book. There are stories of entrepreneurs being scammed out of thousands of dollars for sending lower level Influencers money without contracts in place.

The first rule of thumb if you are going to pay an Iinfluencer to promote your product is to incorporate a contract with their government name not just their social media name.

The second rule of thumb is to understand that no one can promise you sales. The amount you pay Influencers them does not guarantee sales.

A new strategy that may help would be to change your perception of an Influencer. Influencers don't always have 100k followers on social media. The odds of you having an Influencer already in your social media following is very probable. A local (micro) Influencer is just as effective as a national influencer.

Seven Ways to Collaborate With a Local Influencer

1. Cross promote.

2. Barter services.

3. Start a Book Club.

4. Do a LIVE Video together.

5. Make sure your niche market match and offer engaging social media content and contests.

6. Share FREE product for them to review and promote.

7. Affiliate Marketing

Know The Statistics of Sales

Your reader has seen your marketing, filled out the feedback form, and now they are ready to make initial contact with you to inquiring about purchasing a book, product, service, or bundle from you. The email inquiry pops up and what do you do?

Follow Up Statistics

40% of salespeople never follow up.

25% of salespeople only make a second attempt and stop.

12% only make three contacts and stop.

Only 10% of sales people make more than three contacts.

2% of sales are made on the first attempt.

3% of sales are made on the second attempt.

5% of sales are made on the third attempt.

10% of sales are made on the fourth attempt.

80 % of sales are made on the fifth to twelfth attempt.

Statistics given by Josh Letsis on Instagram.

Creating a Street Team

Every promotion needs a team to convey to the public. This team is usually referred to as your "Street Team". As Authors you will need to recruit individuals that will market your book through a variety of media channels.

Your Street Team should consist of your biggest fans and supporters. This group of people should consist of supporters who frequently share, retweet, engage, and invite others to endorse your brand, books, product, and services. Your Street Team objective is to keep your readers engaged and excited about your book, product, or services.

To begin the *PUSH* you must recruit. This requires screening. If you want to screen properly you should begin by creating a form for interested parties to fill out. There are software in the Marketplace that will create a form for you. The beauty of forms are that they can be embedded on your website, social media pages, and email.

You can recruit in person or online. Both have their benefits. The benefit of online is that the record keeping is automatically uploaded. The benefit of in person is that you get to engage personally with your supporters and hear the enthusiasm in their voice.

How To Recruit Your Street Team

Be sure to collect information you'll need to contact them and keep them updated. The basic information include:

- Full Name

- Email Address

- Mailing Address

- Phone Number

If you want to get more thorough ask questions to determine culture fits:

- Are you a part of any other organizations?

- Are you an introvert or extrovert?

- How often do you attend networking events?

Another great piece of information to include:

- Availability

- Region (if you are marketing in multiple cities)

- T-Shirt size

How To Prepare Your Street Team

Now that you have selected your street team you must inform them of your expectations, objectives, and goals.

Creating a Welcome Packet creates a consistent mode of communication. The Welcome Packet may change per book, product or service but the goal is to have an information packet for each promotion.

– Welcome letter

– About Us

– Description of the promotion

– Objective & Goals

– Rules & Regulations

– Duration of promotion

– Coupon codes

– Promotion locations

How To Reward Street Teams

Everyone likes rewards, validation, and recognition. A good promoter knows how to reward their street team for their *PUSH.*

Here are ways to reward your team:

1. FREE Products

2. FREE Training

3. FREE Food

4. Gift cards

5. T-Shirts

6. Money

How To Communicate To Your Street Team

As a self-publisher you will have the responsibility to make sure all communications are clear and centralized. This is where trendy apps will come in handy. We all know the dangers of communication barriers. It can be catastrophic to your book sales. Here are three ways to deliver clear communications during promotions for your Street Team:

1. Remind: School Communication

2. Facebook Groups

3. Google Groups

Profits Over Popularity

In the first chapter we covered discovering your "WHY" for self-publishing a book. If one of your "WHY's" is making a profit, keep reading.

Are you title driven or purpose driven. This question is asked because it will determine which journey is suitable for you.

The amount of money you can make as a self-depends on your mastery of the *PUSH*. You have to promote until shipping and handling occurs. Hopefully you are learning how to *PUSH*. Now it's time to learn how to make money.

Here is the disclaimer there is not a right or wrong way to distribute your book but there is a profitable way and a perceived profitable way. The question is do you want to have profits or popularity? Can you have both? Yes you can, but one has to come before the other and you are in charge of the order.

Some authors market the title of "Best Seller" but what they don't share is that they give it away for FREE to accelerate units sold on major platforms to get the bragging rights of "Best Seller". There is nothing wrong with this strategy if the goal is to land the title. Some believe that having a "Best Seller" title associated with a book will increase sales.

Here are a few things you should know about the title of Best Seller:

1. It's based off of sales not reviews. That means if an Author give their book away for FREE that increase the odds of more downloads. This strategy however does not guarantee that the book will have great content.

2. Each book is assigned to a category. The rankings are category based. To land the Best Seller badge your book must sell the most books in the category compared to all of the titles in the category.

3. Once your book rank Best Seller you will get promoted more by Amazon which will give your book more exposure for frequent book buyers.

4. It's not unheard of for Authors to purchase mass amounts of their titles to secure a best seller status.

An alternative strategy available for self-publishers is starting your pre-order campaign 90 days before launching on your website and collect capital upfront without the title. Now with this strategy you are not celebrated on a national database as a "best seller" with low/no profits but you still promoting nationally and gaining profits.

According to Bowker, Self-Publishing authors grew from 1.2 million in 2017 to 1.6 million in 2018. That is a 40% increase registered ISBN's.

So what does all of this data forecast? It forecast that taking publishing into your own hands is becoming more common and successful. Yes we want your book to gain notoriety but not without the financial rewards. Do you want fame or finances? Once you have warranted a set amount of revenue you can distribute to online retailers to build a campaign to "Best Seller." The benefit's that now you have capital to market on wider spectrum.

When you sell on national retailer sites you have to pay them commission. This commission is communicated in detail when uploading manuscript so you can make an informed decision if this is the right route for you.

Sophisticated Press LLC is not here to tell you which way to go. Our job is to show you how to *PUSH* using either method.

Interviews and Podcasts Etiquette

When you're *PUSH*ing it's important to campaign through interviews on podcast, FB LIVE, Radio, TV, and etc. as a general rule you should prepare to answer the following questions on every interview:

1. Why did you want to be a writer?

2. Can you share what you're currently writing?

3. What do you enjoy most about connecting with readers?

We have seen the horror stories of Authors or Celebrities being misquoted during interviews. Sometimes their words are taken out of context.

Steps you can take to prevent this miscommunication from happening.

- Have a preset of questions to send to the interviewer.

- Have your responses rehearsed.

- Request that you are able to have your videographer present to record the session for social media purposes.

- Have a list of questions or subjects you don't want to be asked or discussed.

- Lastly, it's ok to turn down interviews or reschedule for another time or season.

These same rules apply for Podcast interviews.

How To Request For Podcast Interviews

1. Listen to two of the podcast shows to determine if it's a culture fit.

2. Look at the Podcast website and YouTube page.

3. Answer the following question:

    a. Can I add value to the audience?

4. Contact the host directly.

    a. Don't contact via social media.

    b. Do contact via an email or DM.

5. Only contact the Podcast host if you can add value to the show.

    a. Do their show content match your mission?

6. Keep your pitch brief and explain your expertise.

7. Ask if there are any fees associated for being a guest. Gauge the fee based on, followers, subscriptions, and subscriptions. Podcast fees may be worth the investment depending on downloads.

8. Register on spotaguest.com to get started. Before you do set up an email for all of your FREE eBook downloads and spam mail.

Here is a great template to use when contacting Interviewers:

Hi (Interviewer name, Podcast name, etc.)

My name is (Insert name). I have listened/viewed to a couple of your shows and I would like to be considered to be a guest on the show.

I am (State your title and name of your book, business, product, or service. Next three sentences should inform of the data that shows your book, business product, or service has affected the masses)

With your audience, I would love to add value by discussing any of the following topics for your show:

- Value #1

- Value #2

- Value #3

If you have any questions, or need any other information, please feel free to contact me.

I look forward to hearing from you.

Best,

Shipping & Handling With Care

Self-publishers should have their book on hand in bulk for orders that are purchased through their personal website. When you receive your books they are in a box or plastic wrapping from the printing distributor. Most book orders are in quantity of 100-1000. When mailing your book out to your supporters hear are a few optional cautions to take.

1. Invest in bubble wrap.

2. Purchase plastic sleeves for your book.

3. Visit www.usps.com, create an account, order FREE shipping boxes.

4. Order cardboard mailers from Amazon.com.

The goal is for the book to arrive to the reader without folded corners. If you really want to create a memorable moment with your readers include a thank you note or autographed acknowledgement. Does this extra attention to detail take more time out of your day? But imagine buying a product from your favorite store and the CEO has a personalized THANK YOU notes.

Benefits of USPS.com For Authors

Media Mail® is a cost-effective way to send media and educational materials. This service has restrictions on the type of media that can be sent. From $2.75 at a Post Office.

What can you send using Media Mail?

- Books (at least eight pages)

- Printed music and test materials

- Video and sound recordings

- Printed educational charts

- Medical loose-leaf pages and binders

- Computer-readable media

NOTE: Video games, computer drives, and digital drives do *not* qualify for Media Mail prices.

Rules & Restrictions

- Maximum weight is 70 lbs.

https://www.usps.com/ship/mail-shipping-services.htm

*Media Mail offers a local rate for books and educational materials.

25 *PUSH* Tips

1.   Ask open ended questions to create engagements.

2.   Practice writing weekly (articles, speeches, blogs, etc.).

3.   Create content and headline last.

4.   Embrace criticism and grow from bad comments.

5.   Take a sabbatical and write without any filters.

6.   Join writer groups.

7.   Hire a Professional Graphic Designer.

8.   Stay current on Business apps.

9.   Invest in a speech recorder or simply use your cell phone recorder.

10. Read two books a month. Good Leaders are readers.

11. Never trust your spell checker.

12. Have a second person read the manuscript.

13. Read manuscript out loud.

14. Ask the Editor for a Sample Edit.

15. Ask for referrals from previous post.

16. Create a budget for a professional editor.

17. Classmates or previous professors are great candidates for editing opportunities.

18. Listen to your manuscript on your desktop or laptop.

19. Check for misspelled words:

- a lot/allot

- affect/effect

- can/may

- further/farther

- good/well

- i.e./e.g.

- into/in to

- it's/its

- lay/lie

- less/fewer

- that/who

- their/they're/there

- then/than

- who/whom

- your/you're

20. Don't over edit. Perfection can lead to procrastination.

21. Use Contractions (Don't vs. Do Not).

22. Cut long sentences into two.

23. Remove repetitive phrases.

24. Check your commas when creating lists.

25. Use quotation marks in dialogue

15 Ways To *PUSH* Your Book

1. Podcast

2. Online Course (Tutorials)

3. Workbook

4. Workshop

5. Speaking Engagements

6. Accessories (T-Shirts, Mugs, Notebooks.)

7. Vendor Events (Make sure to invest in a vendor table & Table Cover)

8. Author Landing Page

9. Facebook LIVES

10. Book Clubs

11. Public Libraries

12. Consultations / Coaching

13. YouTube Channel

14. Mentoring

15. Social Media Influencers

About the Author

Renetta Gunn-Stevens, CEO of Sophisticated Press LLC knew at an early age that she was a Trailblazer, Motivational Speaker, and Activation Specialist.

After many successful collaborations with family, friends, and cohorts that resulted in professional advancements, she decided to join the world of Entrepreneurship.

What started off as a published memorial for her birthday ended in a God ordained profession of publishing. She is now a world renown ghost writer, author, and facilitator of a mass variety of self-published books globally and Founder of Sophisticated Press Author Academy (SPAA).

Titles

By

Renetta Gunn-Stevens

A Dad's Redemption

Kingdom Speaking In The Boardroom

10 Ways to Eliminate Debt By Writing

Visit www.sophisticatedpress.com to order these titles.

Booking For Speaking / Training:
Sophisticatedpress@gmail.com

Attn: Booking Department

Office : 630-755-5580

Fax : 630-566-0356

Address: PO Box 831

Elmhurst IL, 60126

www.ingramcontent.com/pod-product-compliance
Lightning Source LLC
Chambersburg PA
CBHW031951190326
41519CB00007B/756